CARING FOR THE WORLD

By Steffi Cavell-Clarke

Our
Values

BookLife
PUBLISHING

©2020
BookLife Publishing Ltd.
King's Lynn
Norfolk PE30 4LS

ISBN: 978-1-83927-828-0

All rights reserved
Printed in Malaysia

Written by:
Steffi Cavell-Clarke

Edited by:
Kirsty Holmes

Designed by:
Daniel Scase

A catalogue record for this book
is available from the British Library.

All facts, statistics, web addresses
and URLs in this book were verified
as valid and accurate at time of
writing. No responsibility for any
changes to external websites or
references can be accepted by
either the author or publisher.

CONTENTS

Words that look like **this** can be found in the glossary on page 24.

WHAT ARE OUR VALUES?

Values are ideas and beliefs that help us to work and live together in a **community**. Values teach us how to behave and how we should **respect** each other and ourselves.

Respecting others

Understanding different faiths

Making your own choices

Being responsible

Our Values

Helping others

Sharing your ideas

Caring for the environment

Listening to others

5

CARING FOR OUR WORLD

Our world is home to over 7 billion people. All those people need food, clean water and shelter. We get everything we need from our planet, so it's important that we care for it and make it a healthy place to live.

Caring for our world means doing things that will help to keep the Earth healthy, such as recycling plastic bottles and turning off lights when they are not needed.

WHY IS IT IMPORTANT?

We need to take care of planet Earth. All living things need **natural resources**, so it is important that we use them carefully without wasting them.

If we all care for our world, then we will make it a safer place to live.

It's important to save Earth's resources so people in the future can have everything that we have now. Animals and plants also need a healthy environment to live in.

POLLUTION

Pollution happens when land, water or air is made unsafe. There are many types of pollution and they all have bad effects on the environment. Pollution can affect humans, animals and plants.

Air pollution is when the air has been **contaminated** by smoke or harmful **gases**.

Land pollution is when the Earth's surface has been contaminated by **waste** or damaged by humans.

Water pollution is when water has been contaminated with waste.

CLEAN AIR

Air pollution is very dangerous to animals, humans and plants. One of the biggest causes of air pollution is the burning of **fossil fuels** and the gases given out by cars and aeroplanes.

Holly had a lesson about air pollution at school. Afterwards, she decided to walk to school with her dad instead of travelling by car. She knew that this would help to look after the environment.

CLEAN WATER

Water covers most of planet Earth. Oceans and seas have salt water, whilst rivers and lakes have fresh water. There is only a small amount of fresh water on Earth, so it is important to save water where we can.

Fresh water is very important. People need to drink it to stay alive and healthy. Here are some simple ways to save water:

- Never leave water running

- Turn off the tap while you brush your teeth

- Take a shower instead of a bath

- Ask an adult to fix dripping taps

RECYCLING OUR RUBBISH

Rubbish is made up of things that we no longer want or need. We create huge amounts of rubbish every day. Rubbish is either buried or burned, which is harmful to the environment. To look after the environment, we can recycle our rubbish.

Recycling is when we turn old things into new things.

Paper, plastic, glass and metal can all be recycled. Ashley always recycles her magazines so that they can be made into new things.

If you see packaging with this sign, it means it can be recycled.

CARING FOR WILDLIFE

There are many **species** of animal that are in danger of becoming **extinct**. This is because humans are destroying their homes in order to get more natural resources.

Humans cut down trees and use the wood to make paper, furniture and buildings. This leaves the animals who live in the trees without a home, so it is important that we plant new trees around the world.

CARING FOR EACH OTHER

Planet Earth is your home too. When it is clean and healthy, the people, plants and animals are healthier too.

The children at Abby's school always put their rubbish in the bin, instead of throwing it on the ground. This means that their environment is clean and healthy.

MAKING A DIFFERENCE

It is important to care for the environment where you live. There are lots of things we can do where we live that will help the whole planet.

Reuse when you can.

Walk or bike to school.

Always put your rubbish in the bin.

Remember these simple ways to help make a difference to your environment:

Switch off electrical things when they are not in use.

Save water by turning off taps.

GLOSSARY

community	a group of people who are connected by something
contaminated	to have made something unclean by adding something harmful or poisonous to it
environment	your surroundings
extinct	when a species of animal is no longer alive
fossil fuels	fuels, such as coal, oil and gas, which formed millions of years ago from the remains of animals and plants
gases	things that are like air, which fill any space available
natural resources	useful materials that are created by nature
respect	thinking good things about (or looking up to) someone or something
responsible	in charge of doing certain things
species	a group of very similar animals or plants that can create young together
waste	things left over that are no longer needed

INDEX

PHOTO CREDITS

Abbreviations: l – left, r – right, b – bottom, t – top, c – centre, m – middle. Images are courtesy of Shutterstock.com. With thanks to Getty Images, Thinkstock Photo and iStockphoto. Front cover – wavebreakmedia. 2 & 3l – Sunny Studio. 4 – Rawpixel.com. 5tl – Monkey Business Images, 5tm – Tom Wang, 5tr – Yuliya Evstratenko, 5mr – Romrodphoto, 5br – Luis Molinero, 5bm – Pressmaster, 5bl – amenic181, 5ml – ESB Professional. 6 – karelnoppe. 7 – wavebreakmedia. 8 – Anna Nahabed. 9 – all_about_people. 10 – Hung Chung Chih. 11t – INSAGO, 11m – branislavpudar, 11b – De Visu. 12 – Toa55. 13 – SimplyDay. 14 – 2xSamara.com. 15 – Nikola Solev. 16 – wavebreakmedia. 17 – Rawpixel.com. 18 – Onyx9. 19 – Mny-Jhee. 20 – Sunny Studio. 21 – Rawpixel.com. 22 – Rawpixel.com. 23tl – Brian A Jackson, 23tm – wavebreakmedia, 23tr – Switlana Symonenko, 23br – Africa Studio, 23bl – TonnaPong.